WASHINGTON
Portrait of a State

WASHINGTON

Portrait of a State

JOHN MARSHALL

GRAPHIC ARTS™ BOOKS

Library of Congress Control Number: 2005929669
International Standard Book Number: 978-1-55868-921-3

Captions and book compilation © MMVI by
Graphic Arts™ Books, an imprint of Graphic Arts Books
P.O. Box 56118
Portland, OR 97238-6118
(503) 254-5591

Dust Jacket Design: Vicki Knapton
Interior Design and Captions: Jean Andrews

Fourth Printing
Printed in China

FRONT COVER: ◖ Situated in the Mount Baker–Snoqualmie
National Forest, Mount Shuksan stretches 9,131 feet above sea level.
BACK COVER: ◖ Snoqualmie Falls is a spectacular 270-foot cascade situated
twenty-eight miles east of Seattle in the foothills of the Cascade Mountains.
◄◄ South of La Push in the Olympic National Park, sea stacks with a topping of
rugged trees rise at Second Beach. The sea stacks are relics of ancient rocky headlands.
◄ Mount Rainier rises beyond Longbranch on Kitsap Peninsula, South Puget Sound.
► In Skagit Valley each spring, tulips are always the headline stars, though they are
preceded by bright yellow daffodils and followed by colorful irises and lilies.

▲ In Okanogan County, the Methow Valley is
Washington's equivalent of the Old West. A drive up the valley
passes big old weathered barns, fields of baled hay, cattle ranches, and
corrals full of horses, as well as glimpses of the high peaks of the Cascades.
▶ Near Dryden, orchard ladders await more temperate weather
when they will be used for pruning trees. At below zero,
the temperature is too cold for outdoor work.

◄ A familiar sight in the Palouse Country, a combine
makes artwork of a wheat field. The combine has made it
possible for a single person to do what would take hundreds to
do by hand. Such equipment costs up to a couple of million dollars.
▲ Rolling hills, planted in wheat, rise behind a farm near Garfield in
Whitman County. Ladow Butte, 3,296 feet high, is in the background.

▲ Apple trees planted beside an irrigation
canal near Parker in the Yakima Valley show fall color.
▶ Palouse Falls, with a drop of 198 feet, is the major
attraction of the 105-acre Palouse Falls State Park.

◄ Poplar windbreaks surround the Auvil
Fruit Company orchards, south of Vantage.
▲ Pediocactus, also known as hedgehog cactus, thrives
in arid areas of the state, usually at elevations of less than a
thousand feet. A scant seven inches of precipitation
fall in parts of the northern desert.

◄ Alpine larch in fall color stands before 8,041-foot Prusik Peak,
reflected in Sprite Tarn in the Enchantment Peaks area near Leavenworth.
▲ Goat Rocks Wilderness, a 105,600-acre alpine wonderland, sports
a colorful wildflower carpet woven of paintbrush, fleabane,
bear grass, lupine, and American bistort.

▲ Coast or Pacific rhododendron *(Rhododendron macrophyllum)* flourishes with western hemlock on Mount Walker in the Olympic National Forest. In 1893, before women had the right to vote, an unusual women-only election chose the rhododendron as the state flower. Fifty-six years later—in 1949— the state legislature officially recognized the women's choice and named the "rhody" Washington's state flower.

▲ The Green River flows through Kanaskat-Palmer
State Park in western Washington. The park's 320 acres
support camping, boat and raft launching, river
rafting, kayaking, trout fishing, and picnicking.

▲ The Mukilteo Lighthouse, established
in 1906, overlooks Puget Sound near the ferry
landing in historic Mukilteo. Housed in the thirty-
foot wooden tower, the original Fresnel lens is still in use.
► The Bellevue Botanical Garden encompasses thirty-six
acres of display gardens, including rolling hills,
woodlands, meadows, and wetlands.

▲ Native American canoe paddlers from
villages of the Puget Sound, the Olympic Peninsula, and
Canada gather with their dugout canoes at Point Defiance Park, Tacoma.
▶ In 1841, Charles Wilkes of the U.S. Exploring Expedition approached a peninsula
near Admiralty Inlet, thinking it was a substantial point. On finding
it was just a small spit, Wilkes designated it Point No Point.
In 1880, a lighthouse was established on the point.

◄ The 605-foot Space Needle, designed
for the 1962 World's Fair, dominates the Seattle skyline.
▲ Washington State Ferries (WSF), the nation's largest ferry transit
system, carries more than twenty-five million people each year. Ferries provide
daily transportation between Seattle (population more than 560,000)
and Bremerton, Bainbridge Island, and Vashon Island.

▲ Olympic National Park is home
to extremes, ranging from glacier-capped mountains to
magnificent forests to the wild Pacific Coast. In the Hoh Rain Forest,
a three-quarter-mile round-trip trail allows access
to the other-worldly Hall of Mosses.

▲ Columbian white-tailed deer browse at Julia
Butler Hansen Refuge for the Columbian White-tailed Deer
in the Lower Columbia River near Cathlamet. The Columbian white-tail
is one of thirty-nine subspecies of the small- to medium-sized white-
tailed deer. The Washington herd is listed as an Endangered
Species with the U.S. Fish and Wildlife Service.

▲ The annual Port Townsend Wooden Boat
Festival is the largest festival for wooden boats on
the West Coast. The Olympic Mountains rise in the background.

▶ The original *Lady Washington* fought to help the colonies gain their independence
from England. The reproduction *Lady Washington,* shown here docked at
the Wooden Boat Festival, played the part of HMS *Interceptor*
in Walt Disney Pictures' *Pirates of the Caribbean.*

◄ The stretch from Shi Shi Beach to La Push is the
wildest section of coastline in the Lower 48 states. Shi Shi maintains its
wildness because of its remote location, accessible only by hiking a rigorous trail.
▲ Mountain goats, native to the Cascades, are perfectly adapted to living on very steep
slopes. They were introduced to the rugged Olympics by people interested in hunting,
but the animals have decimated native plants there. Because of that, efforts
are being made to relocate some of them back to the Cascades.

◄ On Orcas Island, Westsound is a favorite destination
for boaters. The largest of the San Juan Islands, horseshoe-shaped
Orcas Island is also a great place for bicycling. Mount Constitution, rising to
2,409 feet, offers unparalleled vistas of the islands stretching out through the sound.
▲ An aerial view shows a purse seiner fishing for sockeye salmon in the San Juans. A purse
seine is netting with a steel rope running through to enable fishermen to close the net like a purse.
The smaller boat, a skiff, lays the net, then pulls on the larger boat to keep boat and net apart.

▲ San Juan Island is the site of one of America's most interesting
wars—the Pig War. In a boundary dispute, an American shot an Englishman's
pig in 1859. From 1860 to 1872, both the United States and Great Britain occupied the
island. In the end, Kaiser Wilhelm I of Germany arbitrated the dispute, awarding the island
to the United States. If cooler heads had not prevailed, the war's single casualty of a pig
could have escalated into an all-out conflict between the United States and Britain.

▲ Mount Baker towers 10,781 feet above sea level.
As viewed from Lopez Island in the San Juan Islands, the
mountain, situated some fifty miles away, appears to rise directly
from the sea. Lopez Island, fifteen miles long and eight miles
wide, has a year-round population of 2,200 people.

▲ Deception Pass State Park encompasses Deception Pass, a narrows
through which water flows with tremendous force as the tide rises and falls,
creating strong currents. Captain Vancouver coined the name "Deception Pass" when
he realized that what he thought was a peninsula was actually an island.
▶ On San Juan Island, Roche Harbor's marina hosts yachts from
around the world. The quaint town is a step back into
history; some of its buildings date from the 1880s.

◄ An aerial view of the San Juans reveals
why a trip through the islands is a favorite for so
many. Here, two ferryboats approach each other at sunset.
▲ Teenager Rachel Cichowski has just caught a coho salmon
in Admiralty Inlet along the shore of Whidbey Island.

▲ In the Henry M. Jackson Wilderness Area of the Washington
Cascades, a stream flowing underneath a snowbank has formed a cave.
Lake Blanca is perfectly framed through the cave's heart-shaped entrance.
▶ Ice melts from a pond beneath Yellow Aster Butte, situated in the Mount Baker
Wilderness area of the Mount Baker–Snoqualmie National Forest.
Mount Larrabee, 7,861 feet high, is reflected in the water.

◄ A southern look toward Boston Peak from Sourdough Mountain
in the North Cascades National Park reveals Diablo Lake in the Ross Lake
National Recreation Area. The North Cascades Highway is visible along the shore.
▲ Eric Thorson rests at Fern Lake in the Wenatchee National Forest. Alpine
larch *(Larix lyallii)* in fall color adds brilliance to the scene.

▲ Near the town of Twisp (population about 1,000), in the
Sawtooth Mountains, a small lake is surrounded by alpine larch in fall color.
▶ Mountain climber/photographer Cliff Leight hikes along the Chain Lake Trail
in the 11,790-acre Mount Baker Wilderness area. Mount Shuksan,
within North Cascades National Park, rises in the distance.

▲ Pollen cones on ponderosa pine will soon
open and release pollen. When the pollen is released, it
looks like clouds of dust coming off the trees. The pollen cones are
necessary to fertilize the female cones, which we recognize as "pine cones."
The ponderosa *(Pinus ponderosa)* is so named because of its ponderous size.
▶ Lake Chelan, 1,486 feet deep, is the third-deepest lake in North America.
Carved out by a glacier, it is fifty-five miles long.

◄ Six-year-old Sophie Marshall needs
both hands to hold a huge Spokane beauty apple.
▲ A rainbow arcs over the lower Wenatchee Valley near
Monitor. The basically dry area's irrigation system supports
cultivation of apples, pears, cherries, peaches, apricots,
plums, nectarines, and wine grapes.

▲ Powder snow has captured the wing
prints of a bird in a Wenatchee Valley orchard.
▶ Leavenworth is a quaint little Bavarian village
nestled in the central Cascade Mountains.

◄ Washington is the nation's top apple-producing
state. Among the varieties are the imperial gala (shown),
braeburn, cameo, fuji, gala, golden delicious, granny smith, honey
crisp, jonagold, pink lady, and red delicious. Apples are grown commercially
in the Yakima Valley, Columbia Basin, and localized areas of western Washington.
▲ Available almost year-round, the green d'Anjou pear is the most abundant pear variety
in the United States. Here, d'Anjou pears ripen in an orchard near Monitor.

◄ Bunchgrass combines with the rolling hills near
Monitor, in the Wenatchee Valley to create a study of light and shadow.
▲ Wildflowers—arrow-leaf balsamroot *(Balsamorhiza sagittata)* and lupine—
brighten the foothills on the east slope of the Washington Cascades
near Cashmere. Eight different species of lupine, all poisonous
to livestock, are common in the Columbia Basin.

▲ Charles Marshall is surrounded by lupine in Icicle
Canyon near Leavenworth. Icicle Canyon is a destination for wildflower
enthusiasts, as well as rock climbers, who enjoy challenging numerous cliffs and
domes, including Ski Tracks Crack, Whoopsie Pillar, Trundle Dome, and Fridge Boulder.
► Seven-year-old Charles and Theo Marshall enjoy hiking with their dog,
Goldie—and dad—at Eagle Rock in the Wenatchee National Forest.

◄ Conconully, established in 1886 because silver
was discovered nearby, was first named Salmon City. By 1888,
the town had 500 people and became the county seat for Okanogan County.
Today fewer than 200 people live in Conconully, and it is no longer the county seat.
▲ Marked by round bales, a cattle ranch in the South Pine Creek Valley
nestles beneath 5,122-foot-high Funk Mountain.

▲ Cottonwood and aspen trees in fall color
line the banks of the Methow River between Twisp
and Winthrop. The Methow is great for fishing—when it is open.
Salmon and steelhead returning to the Methow must navigate more than
500 miles upriver from the Pacific Ocean, while passing through
nine mainstream Columbia River dams.

▲ Saddle horses winter in the northern
desert on open range south of Wenatchee.
Rounded up each spring, they are ridden by
children at camps in the summer.

▲ An adult osprey brings a fish to its waiting mate
and young at Pend Oreille River in northeast Washington.
▶ The sky becomes an artist's palette as the sun sets on the
Spokane River. The Great Northern Railroad Station
on the left pokes a hole in the composition.

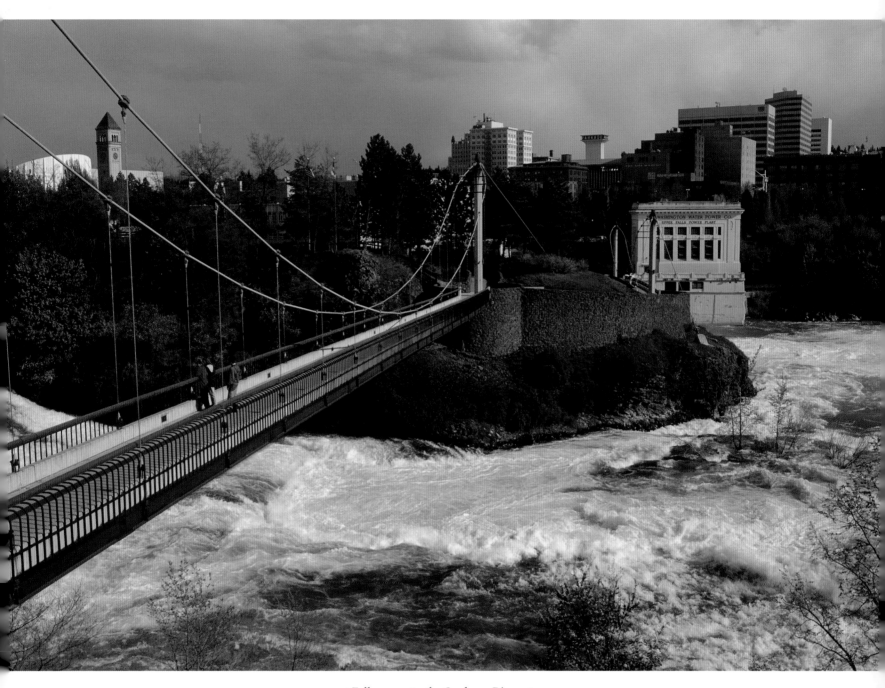

◄ Fall comes to the Spokane River at
Riverside State Park. Basalt, a dark, heavy, iron-rich
and silica-poor volcanic rock, forms the banks of the river.
▲ A footbridge crosses the turbulent waters of the
Spokane River at Riverfront Park in Spokane.

▲ Consisting of ninety acres, Manito Park
in Spokane was originally called Montrose Park. In
1903, its name was changed to *Manito*, which means "Spirit
of Nature" in the dialect of the Algonquin Native American tribe.
▶ Backdropped by lilacs in bloom, a freight wagon and steam
engine reflect the mining history of the town of Republic.

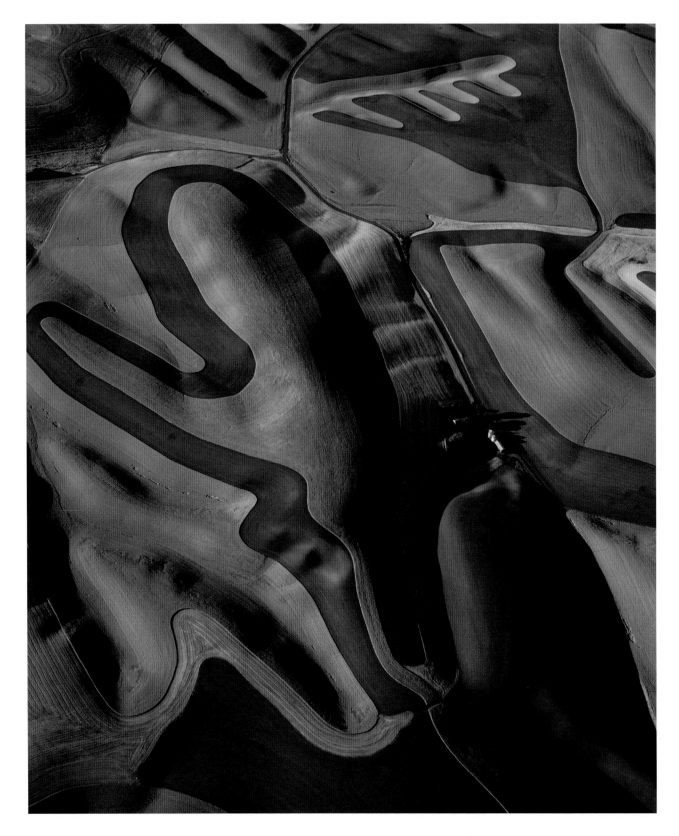

◄ An aerial view of the Palouse Hills in Whitman County shows intricate designs
created by strip farming, a strategy for erosion control. Brown shows fallow ground.
Soil washed off bare ground collects in cultivated areas, rather than being washed away.

▲ A "round" barn near Pullman actually has eight sides. It was restored
in 2000–2001 after a windstorm blew the cupola off the top.

►► Spring brings color to the light-and-shadow designs
of the Palouse Hills south of Colfax.

◄ Though spectacular in spring and summer,
this winter Palouse Falls holds an unusually cold, icy beauty.
▲ Craig Martin rides out, looking for stray cattle
in the Blue Mountains near Dayton.

▲ A covered wagon rests at the Whitman Mission
National Historic Site near Walla Walla on the Oregon Trail.
Red-winged blackbirds *(Agelaius phoeniceus)* observe from a rail fence.
▶ As seen from the air, Grande Ronde River in southeast Washington snakes
its way through the canyon it has carved over millions of years.

◄ Washington ranks first in the nation in sweet
cherry production, averaging 85,000 to 95,000 tons in recent years.
▲ A cherry orchard in Yakima Valley near Naches exhibits the famous cherry blossoms.
►► Called the Eighth Wonder of the World, Grand Coulee Dam, on the Columbia
River, is North America's largest concrete structure. Besides producing
up to 6.5 million kilowatts of power, the dam provides irrigation
for more than five hundred thousand acres of farm land.

75

▲ At Red Willow Vineyard in the Yakima Valley, vines are planted
on a peninsula of land jutting out from the south-facing Ahtanum Ridge.
▶ The Sangiovese wine grape is only one of the numerous varietals pioneered
by Red Willow Vineyard. Others are Syrah, Malbec, Viognier, and
Cabernet Franc. The vineyard has also long produced
award-winning Cabernet Sauvignon and Merlot.

◄ The Beverly Sand Dunes, deposited
by Ice Age floods, encompass some three hundred acres.
▲ The California subspecies of bighorn sheep finds the rugged, arid
Yakima River canyon ideal habitat. Completely wiped out during pioneer
days, bighorn sheep were reintroduced to the area from populations
in British Columbia. Rams are characterized by long, curving
horns. Ewes have much more slender, shorter horns.

81

▲ The wheat harvest on the Waterville Plateau,
elevation 2,000 feet, yields an average of forty to seventy
bushels per acre. Wheat is grown on nearly one-third of all cropland
in Washington and is a valuable part of the state's farm economy.
▶ Wheat and barley are major crops in the area surrounding
Coulee City. Here, railroad tracks lead to a grain silo, used
to store the grain until it can be shipped to market.

▲ Holden Keen snowboards at Mission Ridge.
At an elevation of nearly 7,000 feet, stunted trees, plastered
with windblown snow and rime, or frozen fog, embellish the slopes.
▶ Just seventy-eight miles from Seattle, Stevens Pass is a favorite destination
for snowboard, ski, and cross-country enthusiasts of all ages and abilities. The
highway is visible here, but there is also a 7.8-mile-long railroad tunnel, the longest
in the United States, that makes its way unseen beneath the mountain.

◄ The Wenatchee River offers sections of water to suit just
about everyone's tastes and abilities. This stretch is a major salmon-
spawning area, supporting one of the healthiest chinook runs in the Northwest.
Downstream, whitewater rafters and kayakers find their perfect adventure.
▲ Rick and Terri Halstead enjoy the beauty and peace of canoeing at Lake
Wenatchee State Park. The lake has by far the largest population
of sockeye salmon spawning in the Lower 48 states.

▲ Below the town of Index, a commercial
rafting trip through Boulder Drop on the Skykomish
River provides plenty of excitement. The river is
also a favorite for steelhead fishing.

▲ Mount Rainier National Park hosts the
headwaters of the Paradise River. The mountain rises to
14,410 feet above sea level. It is an active volcano enveloped
in some thirty-five square miles of snow and ice and wrapped
by old-growth forest and incredible wildflower meadows.

▲ A waterfall punctuates the flow on Silver Creek,
in the Wenatchee National Forest near Snoqualmie Pass.
▶ Ponderosa pine, also known as western yellow pine
and bull pine, lines the Hatchery Creek Road.

◀ Pink monkeyflower *(Mimulus lewisii)*
brightens the banks of Snowgrass Creek in the Goat Rocks
Wilderness. A 105,600-acre alpine wonderland, the Goat Rocks Wilderness is
a portion of the volcanic Cascade Range between Mount Rainier and Mount Adams.
▲ A waterfall tumbles down Silver Creek, near Easton in the Snoqualmie
Pass area of the Wenatchee National Forest.

▲ Just a few miles from the town of Leavenworth,
the area around Icicle Creek is marked by seven Forest Service
campgrounds, which are especially popular for summer weekend campouts.
▶ Chikamin Peak, 6,687 feet high, rises above Gold Creek.

◄ A fisherman gets in the last of the season
at Takhlakh Lake in the Gifford Pinchot National
Forest. Mount Adams, 12,307 feet high, is in the background.
▲ Vine maple and bracken fern mingle in a cut-over private forest
near Willard. In open areas, with the right combination of moisture
and temperature, the vine maple may turn a brilliant red in fall,
but where it is sheltered by a forest canopy, it only turns yellow.

97

▲ Weathered snags, killed and bent during the
1980 eruption of Mount St. Helens, still show the effects
of the destructive forces that simmer beneath the mountain.
▶ A healthy elk herd, thriving inside the Mount St. Helens National
Volcanic Monument, demonstrates the recovery that continues
to take place throughout the once-devastated area.

◄ Light rays pass through big-leaf maple
trees *(Acer macrophyllum)* near Castle Rock.
▲ The Church in historic Oysterville was built
in 1892 at a cost of $1,500 and presented to the
Baptist denomination as a gift. The Church
has been nondenominational since 1980.

◄ Near the town of Packwood, a small waterfall accents
Glacier Creek, which flows out of the Goat Rocks Wilderness.
▲ The Little White Salmon River flows through a basalt gorge. The river
combines crystal-clear water with a turbulent mix of steep
boulder gardens, ledges, and waterfalls.

▲ In Goat Rocks Wilderness near White Pass,
powder snow decorating trees and blown into drifts has
created odd shapes. Centrally located in the middle of the state, White Pass
Ski Resort offers skiing for all skill levels, including downhill and cross-country.
► On a clear morning following a winter storm, Goat Rocks Wilderness near
White Pass in the Washington Cascades looks like something fairies
have created. The trees are covered with snow and rime.

◄ Historically, in the late spring of every year
the fur brigades returned to Fort Vancouver from the far
reaches of the West. Today, volunteers in authentic period dress reenact
those historic days during the annual Brigade Encampment at Fort Vancouver.
▲ Centralia, historically a logging and railroad town, has recently embraced its historical look.
►► Tadd Wheeler and Kacie L. Jorgensen Schilz canoe in the Tilton Arm
of Mayfield Lake, in Ike Kinswa State Park.

▲ Western sandpipers rest on a mudflat at high tide in Bowerman Basin, a small bay
in Gray's Harbor. The birds regularly stop here to feed and rest during spring migration.
► Seventy-nine-year-old Wilmer Johnson hauls a spring chinook salmon aboard his wooden gill-net
boat. Salmon entering the mouth of the Columbia River swim upriver as far as central Idaho.
►► North Head Lighthouse, in Cape Disappointment State Park, began full operations
in 1898. The lantern room is 65 feet from the ground and 194 feet above sea level.
Winds at North Head have been clocked at more than 100 miles per hour.